TEACHERS GUIDE

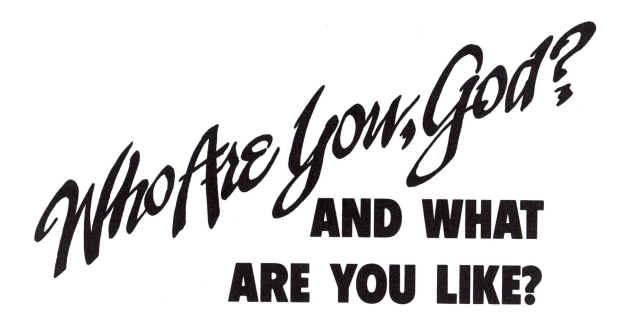

Who Are You, God?

AND WHAT ARE YOU LIKE?

DAWSON McALLISTER **RAY PRITCHARD**

Verses marked (TLB) are taken from *The Living Bible*, © 1971 by the Tyndale House Publishers, Wheaton, IL. Used by permission.

Verses marked (NIV) are taken from *The Holy Bible: New International Version*, © 1978, 1983 by the New York International Bible Society, and are used by permission of Zondervan Bible Publishers.

Verses marked (NKJV) are taken from *The New King James Version*, © 1979, 1980, 1982, Thomas Nelson Inc., Publishers.

Verses marked (NASB) are from the *New American Standard Bible*, © The Lockman Foundation 1960, 1962, 1963, 1968, 1971, 1972, 1973, 1975, 1977.

Verses marked (TEV) are from *Today's English Version*, © 1983 by Thomas Nelson, Inc. and used by permission.

The use of selected references from various versions of the Bible in this publication does not necessarily imply publisher endorsement of the versions in their entirety.

Printed in the United States of America ISBN 0-923417-13-3

SHEPHERD MINISTRIES
2845 W. Airport Freeway, Suite 137
Irving, Texas 75062
(214) 570-7599

CONTENTS

INTRODUCTION

Congratulations! You have one of the highest privileges given to teachers of God's Word -- the privilege and responsibility of teaching God's truth to students.

You may be a pastor, a Sunday School teacher, a youth pastor, a Christian school teacher, a volunteer youth leader or a parent. But whatever role you're in, God wants to use you in touching students for Him. Can you think of any task more important than helping today's students grasp the solutions to their needs?

Never before have students needed God's answers more than today. Their thoughts and standards are being bombarded constantly by the philosophy and thinking of today's godless society. Every day students are being exposed to humanism, selfishness and hopelessness, with the tragic results evident everywhere.

Youth must know what God says about life if they are to withstand the pressures of the evil that surrounds them. You can be a key person in helping them come to grips with God's answers; you can help students obey God on a day-to-day basis through the power of the Holy Spirit.

No one ever said teaching youth was easy; it is not! They will challenge your resources, question your knowledge and test your faith. But through God's power you can effectively teach youth. It is our prayer that this teacher's guide will help you to be the best communicator that you can be to the youth God brings to your life.

Dawson McAllister and Ray Pritchard

USING THE
TEACHER'S GUIDE

We have designed this *Teacher's Guide* to accompany the manual *Who Are You God, and What Are You Like?* by Dawson McAllister and Rich Miller. It has been written with the assumption that you as a teacher will have a copy of the student manual in hand as you prepare each lesson. In order to make your teaching effort more effective, we strongly recommend that each student have his own copy of the discussion manual.

There are several points which will help you be a more effective teacher:

1. <u>Be sure to take the time to read the manual.</u>

It would be a big mistake to begin your preparation by studying the *Teacher's Guide*. You will be much better off to start by going through the manual itself, completing the various questions and projects, and making teaching notes in the margins. Once you have done that, the *Teacher's Guide* will be much more useful to you.

2. <u>Be sure to give yourself enough time to prepare each lesson.</u>

You will find that the lesson plans in this *Teacher's Guide* are chock full of good ideas. However, many of them involve projects which cannot easily be assembled at the last minute. Some of them, in fact, will require preparation several weeks in advance. Therefore, it would be helpful if you read through the entire *Teacher's Guide* before beginning the first lesson. That way you won't be caught by surprise when you come across a good idea you can't use because the first time you read it was 10:30 P.M. on Saturday night!

3. <u>Feel free to tailor each lesson to your own requirements.</u>

The lesson plans are meant as suggestions, not as rules to follow. Most of the lessons contain more material than you will need. Therefore, it isn't necessary that you try to teach everything. Furthermore, some teaching ideas work better in some settings than they do in others. Feel free to add or subtract as you see fit. Your students will appreciate your personal touch.

4. <u>Remember that prayer is the most essential ingredient in effective teaching.</u>

Nowhere is that truth more evident that when you attempt to teach others about the nature and character of God. To teach the truth about God to man is the highest and noblest kind of teaching. To do it well requires a keen mind and an open heart. Do not make the mistake of thinking that prayer and preparation are two different things. When you teach about God, prayer <u>is</u> preparation.

FALSE IDEAS PEOPLE HAVE ABOUT GOD

RELATES TO STUDENT MANUAL PAGES 4-15

INTRODUCTION:

This lesson will set the stage for the whole course. In essence, you will be discussing four false views of God. The point you want the students to grasp is that there actually are people who believe these false views. You don't need to worry about giving an answer to these various ideas. In a sense, everything that follows this lesson is a detailed, biblical "answer." That is, the answer to a false view of God is to get a biblical view of who God really is. Therefore, anything you can do to stir up discussion in this first lesson will be a good thing.

At the end of this session, your students should:

- *Be challenged by the notion that many of their friends have false views of God.*

- *Be excited about the opportunity they have to learn about who God really is.*

HOOK:

The student discussion manual offers on page five a sampling of responses by actual students to the question, "What is God like?" Why not have your students conduct their own survey? A few days before the class, ask 4 or 5 students to do an informal survey at school with the question, "What is God like?"

A variation on this would be to take a tape recorder to a shopping mall or to a downtown street and tape the actual responses to that question.

Either one of these projects will take some preparation but the diversity of answers you get will more than repay the effort. It is important that your students see for themselves that there are many different views of God--even among their friends at school.

An excellent follow-up would be to ask your students to complete the question on page 5, "How would you describe God?" Give them 60 seconds and tell them they must answer the question in 20 words or less. The results may surprise you.

Even among teenagers who have been raised in the church there is a widespread ignorance of who God really is. Most have never seriously studied the attributes and character of God. **This series -- <u>Who is Your God and What is He Like?</u> -- will be new material to most of your students.**

Explain that before you begin studying who God really is, it will help to understand some of the false ideas people have about God. "In this lesson, you will learn about four of the most popular false ideas."

KEY PRINCIPLES FROM CHAPTER ONE:

> *1.   THE MOST OBVIOUS FALSE IDEA ABOUT GOD IS THE BELIEF THAT THERE IS NO GOD AT ALL.*
>
> *2.   A SECOND FALSE IDEA ABOUT GOD IS THE BELIEF THAT GOD MAY EXIST, BUT CAN NEVER BE KNOWN.*
>
> *3.   ANOTHER FALSE IDEA ABOUT GOD IS THE BELIEF THAT GOD IS WEAK AND PERMISSIVE.*
>
> *4.   THE MOST POPULAR FALSE IDEA ABOUT GOD IS THAT HE IS AN ANGRY "COSMIC KILLJOY" DETERMINED TO MAKE LIFE MISERABLE.*

Key Principle # 1: THE MOST OBVIOUS FALSE IDEA ABOUT GOD IS THE BELIEF THAT THERE IS NO GOD AT ALL.

■ Ask your students how many true atheists they have known. As the manual notes, most people believe in some form of higher being.

■ The key text is Romans 1:19-20. It establishes that even without the Bible men can look at the world around them and see clear evidence that there is a God who created the world. Spend some time on the point that "God has put this knowledge in their hearts." If God has put this knowledge in the heart of every man, how can there be atheists?

■ The point is, it's hard to be an atheist because it means denying the obvious evidence of creation **and** the truth God has put in the heart of every man. That explains why:

A. There aren't many true atheists, and why

B. Most atheists are very outspoken.

They have to speak out boldly to counteract the obvious evidence for God. If they were quiet, they might have to admit that God exists!

■ Read Psalm 14:1-3 and ask, "What does God say about those who deny his existence?"

3

■ The next question, "Why do you think atheists work hard to try to disprove God's existence?", is an excellent one for discussion.

■ Summarize by making the crucial point that those who deny God's existence do so for moral and spiritual reasons and not because of a lack of evidence. They deny God because they don't want to have to deal with Him.

Key Principle # 2: A SECOND FALSE IDEA ABOUT GOD IS THE BELIEF THAT GOD MAY EXIST, BUT CAN NEVER BE KNOWN.

■ This idea sounds technical, but actually is fairly common. It describes the man or woman who says, "Yes, I'm sure there's a God, but I don't bother Him and He doesn't bother me."

■ The manual implies several reasons people have for taking that position:

A. They think there is nothing to gain by knowing God.

B. They care only about what they can get from God.

C. They don't want to make any personal commitment to God.

D. They think it's God's fault that they don't know Him better.

■ Write those four reasons on an overhead. Then divide your students into four groups. Let each group discuss how they would answer a person who gave that reason for ignoring God.

Key Principle # 3: ANOTHER FALSE IDEA ABOUT GOD IS THE BELIEF THAT GOD IS WEAK AND PERMISSIVE.

■ The key to this section is to understand that it describes a person who believes that God will overlook his sin. In fact, there are millions of people who fit into this general category. To use a term from the classroom, they think God grades on the curve.

■ The passage from Isaiah 29 merits a good explanation by the teacher. Remind the class that God not only sees what we do, He also sees the things we try to cover up.

4

■ **Project:** You are talking one day to a good friend at school. The subject drifts around to dating and your friend strongly implies that he has been "going all the way" with his girl friend. When you start to say something in reply, he just laughs and says, "Hey man, don't worry about me. God and me got something worked out. He knows I'm just having a little fun." Just then the bell rings. You have only a few seconds to get to class. What do you say to your friend?

Key Principle # 4: THE MOST POPULAR FALSE IDEA ABOUT GOD IS THAT HE IS AN ANGRY "COSMIC KILLJOY" DETERMINED TO MAKE LIFE MISERABLE.

■ As the manual notes, the people in this category are on the opposite end from those who think God is weak and permissive. Very often, people who view God as angry and vindictive have suffered a great deal of pain. Their view of God is born out of a tragedy that ripped apart the fabric of life.

■ Complete the exercise on Job 7:12-21. Was Job justified in the things he said? Aren't there times when even the most fervent believer feels this way?

■ **Project:** Ask the students to list some things that can make a person believe that God is angry at them. Then ask, "When was the last time you were angry at God? Why? What happened?"

■ In a sense, the teacher's job in this section is to stir up the students to do some creative thinking about how they feel about God. Let the discussion roll on without trying to bring it to quick "spiritual" ending.

APPLICATION:

■ There are several different ways of wrapping things up depending on what you want to emphasize.

■ Here is one way that will leave your kids hanging. . . . and then will bring them back next week. Try role-playing the four false views of God. That is, take them out of the realm of theory and give them some flesh and blood.

5

■ An elaborate way would be to finish the lesson and tell the students that you have some people you would like them to meet. One by one they enter the room and give a 3 minute "testimony":

An atheist who truly believes there is no God.
An agnostic who believes God doesn't matter.
A hedonist who believes God will let him get away with anything.
An angry person who believes God is out to get him.

Obviously you would have to meet with each person in advance, work out a basic script, and go over the entrance and exit carefully. It's a lot of work, but if done well would leave your students on the edge of their seats.

■ You could accomplish the same thing on a lesser scale by asking four students to role play the parts. It would be helpful to write out a brief paragraph so the students have something to work with.

■ How does such a lesson end? Not with group prayer, silent prayer, or anything meditative. Just tell your group, "The four people you have seen represent millions of other people who are confused or unsure or just plain wrong about God. Beginning next week we're going to find out who God really is."

PRAYER:

"Thank you, Father, for revealing Yourself to us. Open our eyes that we might see You as You are. Amen."

YOUR GOD MUST BE STRONG

RELATES TO STUDENT MANUAL PAGES 16-25

INTRODUCTION:

With this lesson we begin our exploration of the various attributes of God. It might be helpful to get an overview of where we are going. The next four lessons discuss four attributes of God which make Him completely different from us:

Lesson 2 - "YOUR GOD MUST BE STRONG" - Omnipotence

Lesson 3 - "YOUR GOD MUST KNOW EVERYTHING" - Omniscience

Lesson 4 - "YOUR GOD MUST BE BIG" - Omnipresence

Lesson 5 - "YOUR GOD MUST BE IN CONTROL" - Sovereignty

It will be helpful to stress to your students that these attributes are sometimes hard to understand precisely because they describe how God is different from us. Explain to them that they will no doubt have many questions and that the Bible gives us answers to many -- but not all! -- of them. *That is, the Bible tells us everything we __need__ to know about God's attributes, but not necessarily everything we __want__ to know.* Some things are simply beyond our knowledge and are not revealed because we couldn't understand them even if we did know the answer.

The point of saying all this is to assure your students that it is perfectly all right to have questions about who God is. The lessons you are about to teach will help to answer many of them.

HOOK:

The picture on page 16 of the student manual is an excellent place to begin. Have your students pair off and study it for a few moments. Ask them, "What does this picture mean? How can a person's God be too small? Do some people really have a God-in-the-box?" Then ask, "What difference does it make how big your God is?"

With the answers to that question, begin a chart labeled, "The bigger my God is . . ." After just a few seconds of thought, your students should come up with several good answers, e.g., ". . . the more I can trust Him when things are falling apart", and ". . . the more I need to worship Him as God."

Springboard from those answers into the lesson for today. Explain that there are three attributes of God that relate in various ways to God's greatness. They are three "omni" attributes -- Omnipotence, Omniscience, and Omnipresence. Each one gives us an important part of the picture about how great and how big our God really is! An entire lesson will be devoted to each.

The first "omni" attribute is **omnipotence**, which means that God is all-powerful. The manual defines it this way: *God's power is His ability to act with total authority and strength to accomplish His purposes.*

KEY PRINCIPLES FROM CHAPTER TWO:

---

1. *GOD'S POWER IS SO AWESOME IT IS IMMEASURABLE.*

2. *GOD'S POWER IS SO AWESOME NOTHING IS TOO DIFFICULT FOR HIM.*

3. *GOD'S POWER IS SO AWESOME NO ONE OR NOTHING CAN HINDER HIM.*

4. *GOD'S POWER IS SO AWESOME EVERYONE SHOULD PRAISE HIM.*

Key Principle # 1: GOD'S POWER IS SO AWESOME IT IS IMMEASURABLE.

■ The manual is making two simple points in this section:

    A. All power comes from God

    B. His power is without limit

■ Take a few moments to explain the meaning of Psalm 62:11. The ultimate source of all power in the universe is God Himself. All other power is derivative -- it comes from Him. When you flip a switch, a light comes on. The light comes on because the electricity flows to the bulb. The electricity flows through the lines that stretch many miles to a "power plant." The power plant generates its power through giant turbines run by water or fired by coal or by nuclear energy. But the raw materials -- the water, coal, natural gas, or uranium -- those raw materials come ultimately from the hand of God. The "power plant" doesn't make power; it merely transfers it from one form to another. All the power in the universe is like that. It all ultimately comes from God.

■ **Project:** If you have a good-natured student who is into weight-lifting, you might try this: Bring in a set of weights and let him begin lifting at a lower weight, stopping occasionally to add more weight. After the oohs and ahs and the inevitable jokes have died down, the class will watch as he slowly comes to the end of his strength. When he is finished, give him a gift certificate to the local ice cream parlor (to help replenish his strength!) and then point out that all human strength **always** runs out.

■ At this point read Genesis 17:1 and ask your students what the phrase "God Almighty" means. Most of them will have only heard it as a kind of swear word. But the phrase is very significant: It means that God is the All-Mighty One. There is no one greater than He because His strength **never** runs out.

Key Principle # 2: **GOD'S POWER IS SO AWESOME NOTHING IS TOO DIFFICULT FOR HIM.**

■ The exercise on page 20 of the student manual is an excellent place to begin this section. Simply read the two introductory paragraphs and give your students several minutes to complete the exercise.

■ The principle itself is spelled out in Jeremiah 32:17. Read it and ask your students, "According to this verse, how did God create the universe?" Answer: He created it by His power and His outstretched arm.

■ Psalm 33:6,9 gives us another answer to that same question. What is it? Answer: He spoke and the universe came into being.

■ This offers a good chance to bridge back to the early chapters of Genesis. According to chapters 1-2, God created the world in six days. But clearly He didn't have to take six days. He could have created the whole universe in six minutes, or six seconds.

■ That answers one question: Was God tired when He "rested" on the seventh day? (Genesis 2:1-2) No, because he merely spoke and the worlds were formed. God is never tired because His strength never diminishes. He "rested" on the seventh day because the great work of creation was done, not because He was tired.

■ If you have time, you may want to discuss with your students the question on page 21, "What would happen to the universe if God spoke a word against it?" It's a vital question because it points out that our ultimate security rests not in nuclear weapons, but in the Lord Himself. The universe exists by His word; if He spoke a different word, He could make it to disintegrate.

Key Principle # 3: GOD'S POWER IS SO AWESOME NO ONE OR NOTHING CAN HINDER HIM.

■ Note: You may want to spend less time on this section because it is covered in greater detail in Lesson 5 -- "Your God Must be in Control."

■ Page 23 includes a fascinating quotation from Psalm 2. As a way of introducing it, ask your students how they think God feels when evil men fight against Him. Read the passage slowly, pausing at the phrase "But God in heaven merely laughs!"

■ Explain that God "laughs" at the puny efforts of men to overthrow Him. It's like a mouse trying to wrestle an elephant. The odds are stacked in the elephant's favor.

■ Point out that this truth ought to encourage us. There are many situations where your students feel intimidated by the people around them. But God is not intimidated at all by the schemes of the wicked. Point out that if the Lord isn't frightened by such people, then why should we be intimidated? Maybe we can't laugh like God, but we can smile inwardly knowing that God will have the last word.

Key Principle # 4: GOD'S POWER IS SO AWESOME EVERYONE SHOULD PRAISE HIM.

■ Read the introductory sentences of this section. Then have your students Psalm 105:1-2 in unison.

■ Give your students 60 seconds to write down the two or three things about God's power that have impressed them the most.

■ Move from that directly into the application.

APPLICATION:

■ There are several ways to approach the application. Whichever way you choose, be sure to leave enough time to handle it adequately.

■ One way is to close with a time of sentence prayers focused on thanking God for His power and strength.

■ Another approach would be to save the "GOD'S ANSWER TO MY PROBLEM" PROJECT (pages 21-22) until this section. Give each student a few minutes to fill it out. Close with a time of silent prayer as the students commit their problems to God for His solutions.

■ A third way would be to divide into groups and allow your students to work together on writing a contemporary Psalm of praise to God for His greatness. You might read a couple of good examples to help them get started.

■ A final approach would be to list together some of the evidences of God's greatness that the students see around them. Close by singing several worship choruses that focus on God's character. Or, if you focus on the drawing on page 25, you could very naturally sing, "He's Got the Whole World in His Hands."

PRAYER:

"Lord, we know you are bigger than the biggest of our problems. Help us to remember that this week. Amen."

YOUR GOD MUST KNOW EVERYTHING

RELATES TO STUDENT MANUAL PAGES 27-37

INTRODUCTION:

This particular lesson is a study of God's **omniscience,** the fact that "He knows everything about everything." Before you teach it, study the structure of the chapter carefully. The manual breaks **omniscience** into two parts:

God's knowledge -- He knows everything about everything.

God's wisdom -- He knows the best way to accomplish His plans.

The first two key principles deal with God's knowledge, while the last two deal with God's wisdom.

There is a further division within those categories. In both cases the discussion begins with creation and goes to the individual:

God's knowledge --	Details of creation	Point #1
	Details of my life	Point #2
God's wisdom --	Seen in creation	Point #3
	Seen in my body	Point #4

Depending on the time available, you may wish to cover this lesson in two sessions. If you decide to teach it all in one session, be sure to leave enough time at the end for a summary and a strong application.

HOOK:

Here is a simple way to begin. Play a game of Trivial Pursuit with your students. Divide your class into two groups. You act as moderator, asking the questions to each group in turn. You can use the questions from the board game or from any of the various biblical trivia versions. Or you can make up your own. The source of the questions doesn't matter. The key is to begin with a few easy ones and work your way into questions that are extremely obscure or difficult. Eventually every member of both groups will be stumped.

At this point congratulate the students on how much they know. Then point out that even if you had the world's greatest geniuses in the room, even they would be eventually stumped. Why? Because no one knows the answers to every question.

No one, that is, except God. He not only knows all the answers; he knows all the questions. And He's never been stumped yet. That is what **omniscience** is all about. *Omniscience means that God knows everything about everything.*

KEY PRINCIPLES FROM CHAPTER THREE:

---

1. GOD'S KNOWLEDGE IS SO VAST IT INCLUDES ALL THE DETAILS OF CREATION.

2. GOD'S KNOWLEDGE IS SO VAST IT INCLUDES ALL THE DETAILS OF MY LIFE.

3. GOD'S WISDOM IS SEEN IN CREATION.

4. GOD'S WISDOM IS SEEN IN MY BODY.

Key Principle # 1: GOD'S KNOWLEDGE IS SO VAST IT INCLUDES ALL THE DETAILS OF CREATION.

■ The key to teaching this section is in finding a way to help your students grasp the immensity of creation. There are several possibilities:

A. You might ask one of your students who enjoys doing research to prepare a brief report on "How big is the universe?" Such a report should be 3-5 minutes in length and will simply reinforce the point on page 29 that there are billions and billions of galaxies, each with billions and billions of stars.

B. You could show a clip from a documentary film dealing with the stars. (Such films are usually obtainable from your local public library for a very nominal fee.)

C. You might go another route and bring a gallon jar filled with sand. Ask the students to try to count the grains of sand in just one teaspoon.

■ It is worth the effort -- whatever method you use -- to help your students *feel* how great, how vast, and how awesome the universe actually is. It is only against that backdrop that they will appreciate God's **omniscience**.

■ Having established that fact, spend some time on Isaiah 40:26. Ask your students how many people they know by name. Compare that with God who knows the names of billions and billions of stars.

■ If you have the time, complete the "HOW MUCH DOES GOD KNOW" PROJECT on pages 29-30.

Key Principle # 2: GOD'S KNOWLEDGE IS SO VAST IT INCLUDES ALL THE DETAILS OF MY LIFE.

■ Read Psalm 139:1-4 in unison.

■ Make a chart entitled, "Things God Knows About Me." Write in the answers from this passage and then ask the students for additional suggestions. Encourage them to be creative -- e.g., "He knows the flavor of ice cream I'll be eating on July 4 in the year 2019."

■ The two questions at the bottom of page 31 are <u>very important</u>. Make sure you take time to discuss them with your students.

■ Summarize by reading the first paragraph on page 32.

Key Principle # 3: GOD'S WISDOM IS SEEN IN CREATION.

■ At this point, tell your students that you are shifting gears from God's <u>knowledge</u> to God's <u>wisdom</u>. What is the difference between the two? <u>Knowledge</u> is the accumulation of facts about a particular subject. <u>Wisdom</u> is the ability to use the knowledge that you have in the best possible way. <u>Knowledge</u> is what you know; <u>wisdom</u> is what you do with what you know.

■ The great point to stress is that God not only knows everything about everything, but He also knows how to use that unlimited knowledge in the best possible way.

16

■ Perhaps the best way to teach this material is to quickly summarize Proverbs 3:19 and the points made on page 33.

■ Spend a few minutes having your students complete the "LOOK WHAT GOD DID IN HIS WISDOM" PROJECT on page 33.

■ **Illustration**: Suppose you were given a puzzle of 1,000,000 pieces and each piece was different in shape and color from every other piece. And suppose you <u>were not</u> given a picture of what the final design was to look like. How long would it take you to put it all together? Most people wouldn't even try. But that's a tiny picture of what God did when he "put the universe together." He not only designed the pieces (knowledge); He also put them together in an exact fit (wisdom).

Key Principle # 4: GOD'S WISDOM IS SEEN IN MY BODY.

■ The manual quotes Psalm 139:14 as a theme verse for this section. That verse is part of a larger paragraph (verses 13-16) describing God's personal involvement in the development of an unborn child.

■ You might want to show a clip from a film showing the development of an unborn child from conception until the moment of birth. Your local Christian bookstore or your Christian film distributor would no doubt have several such films in stock. A local pro-life support group is another good resource.

■ Another possibility is to make a chart entitled, "My Body at Work." Simply list all the different things that are happening in your body at any given moment, e.g., "Blood is flowing, muscles tensing and relaxing, skin is perspiring, eyes are focusing, sound is being transmitted to the brain." After you make the list, simply comment that at any given moment there are hundreds of other things happening in your body of which you aren't even aware. But God knows all about it. His wisdom is seen in the complex -- yet perfect -- design of the human body.

APPLICATION:

■ Most teenagers spend a lot of time and energy worrying about things -- boy friends, girl friends, homework, problems at home, how they look, what other people think about them, what they are going to do when they graduate, and so on.

■ The truth of God's **omniscience** certainly touches all these areas. Go back to those two **very important** questions on page 31. Also ask the students, "What difference will it make in your life this week that God knows all your past, present and future?"

■ Challenge them to think it out this way. If God already knows what I'm going to do before I do it, and if God has a wise plan for how my life should work out, what am I worried about?

■ Challenge them to pick out one thing that they normally would worry about -- just one thing -- and decide that instead of worrying about it, they are going to trust God in that <u>one specific area</u> this week.

PRAYER:

"Thanks, Lord, for knowing us so intimately and yet loving us so greatly. Amen."

YOUR GOD
MUST BE
BIG

RELATES TO STUDENT MANUAL PAGES 38-45

INTRODUCTION:

This is the final lesson on the three "omni" attributes--**Omnipotence** ("YOUR GOD MUST BE STRONG," Lesson 2), **Omniscience** ("YOUR GOD MUST KNOW EVERYTHING," Lesson 3), and **Omnipresence** ("YOUR GOD MUST BE BIG," Lesson 4).

Your students may find **Omnipresence** the most difficult of the three to grasp. To say that God is present everywhere raises some difficult questions. For instance, how can God be everywhere at once and also be in Heaven? If God is everywhere, does that mean He is in some sense also present in Hell? In what sense did Jesus possess the attribute of **omnipresence** while He was on the earth?

These are good questions and the theological textbooks contain long discussions of the various possible answers. Part of our problem with **omnipresence** is that we have nothing in our own experience to compare with it. That is, when we talk about God being all-powerful, we understand the concept because we ourselves have power and strength. Or when we talk about God being all-knowing, we understand because we ourselves possess knowledge about many things. Even though our power and knowledge is limited, it helps us understand who God is because what we possess in a tiny portion, He possesses in unlimited measure.

It is not so with **omnipresence**. There is no sense in which we can be present everywhere. In fact, there is no way we can be even two places at once!

But God is everywhere at the same time. No wonder we have trouble understanding this attribute. It is totally unlike our present experience.

Because of this, the teacher is well-advised to spend extra time preparing this lesson. Your students will no doubt have many questions about what **omnipresence** means.

HOOK:

The "Voice of the Lord" Game. Have one of your students volunteer to leave the room while everyone else rearranges the furniture. Move the chairs and tables into a bewildering maze. Blindfold the volunteer, bring him back in, and tell him that you will be the "voice of the Lord". Let him know that he can trust you to tell him the right way to go. When the volunteer enters the room, have the other students shout wrong directions. Meanwhile, you should walk next to him, quietly and calmly giving him the right directions.

Play the game with several different volunteers. The moral is obvious: Life is like a maze and there are thousands of voices shouting at us. But no matter where we are, God is right beside us and if we will listen, He will tell us the right way to go. (This game is taken from Group Growers, (Group Books: Loveland, Co., 1988), pp. 102-103.

Tell your students that in this lesson they will learn about the attribute of God that guarantees that He will always be there when they need Him.

KEY PRINCIPLES FROM CHAPTER FOUR:

---

1. GOD'S OMNIPRESENCE MEANS THAT HE IS EVERYWHERE.

2. GOD'S OMNIPRESENCE MEANS THAT HE IS AN INFINITE SPIRIT.

3. GOD'S OMNIPRESENCE MEANS GREAT COMFORT FOR THOSE WHO KNOW AND LOVE HIM.

Principle # 1: GOD'S OMNIPRESENCE MEANS THAT HE IS EVERYWHERE.

■ Spend some time discussing the definition of **omnipresence** on page 39.

■ The story about the Russian cosmonaut is actually quite famous. Ask your students how they would answer his statement.

■ The key Scripture for this entire lesson is Psalm 139:7-12. Have one of the students read it and then as a group answer the first question on page 40.

■ The second question on page 40 is more interesting. Divide your class into small groups and have them suggest possible answers. Encourage your students to think of some places that people would not normally associate with the presence of God. As each answer is mentioned, write it on an overhead or on a blackboard. Then beside each entry, write "HE IS THERE."

■ Reaffirm that **omnipresence** means that God is present everywhere whether we realize it or not and even whether we believe it or not.

(Transition: Read the paragraph at the top of page 41)

Principle # 2: GOD'S OMNIPRESENCE MEANS THAT HE IS AN INFINITE SPIRIT.

■ The great point this section seeks to make is that God is everywhere even though we do not see Him with our eyes. Stress that there are many things we do not see with our eyes that we nevertheless take for granted. The manual offers the example of air -- the odorless, tasteless, invisible substance that surrounds the earth. There are two great lessons from this illustration:

A. We take the existence of air for granted even though we cannot see it.

B. We depend on it for our every existence even though we cannot see it.

Both lessons apply to the existence of God. We take His existence for granted **and** we depend on Him for our existence even though we cannot see him.

■ **Project:** The second example offered by the "HOW CAN GOD BE EVERYWHERE" PROJECT (page 42) is sound waves. Here is a project that will bring the point home to your students. Set up a number of radios before class with their dial settings tuned to different stations. At the appointed moment, ask someone to turn the radios on one by one. Soon a cacophony of discordant sounds will fill the room. Then turn the radios off one by one. Make the point that all those sound waves -- plus hundreds of others (TV, microwave, short-wave transmissions) -- were already in the room. They are there whether we hear them or not. A room that seems to be filled with silence is actually filled with hundreds of voices talking and singing. The reason we don't hear them is because we don't have a receiver tuned in to the right frequency.

■ The application is obvious. Many people mistakenly think that God is far away because they are tuned to the wrong frequency. They think He is silent when actually He is speaking to them all the time.

■ If you use this illustration, simply ask your students how a person tunes in to God's frequency. Answer: By reading the Bible -- **God's Word** --and by coming in faith to Jesus Christ -- **God's Son.**

22

Principle # 3: GOD'S OMNIPRESENCE MEANS GREAT COMFORT FOR THOSE WHO KNOW AND LOVE HIM.

■   Review what **omnipresence** means: God is present everywhere at every moment. There is no place I can go where He is not. In fact, He is there before I get there and He will be there after I leave.

■   The manual draws two conclusions from the truth of God's **omnipresence**:

A.   **Since God is everywhere, He is with me in the hard times.** (Page 44)

■   Read Psalm 37:23-24 and have your students discuss the question at the bottom of page 44, "What does Psalm 37 say God does when we fall?" Answer: He holds us with his hand so that although we may stumble, we will not fall and be destroyed.

■   TESTIMONY: Depending on how much time you have available, you may want to ask one of your students to share briefly how God helped him through a difficult time. If you do this, be sure to arrange the testimony ahead of time so you don't put anyone on the spot.

B.   **Since God is everywhere, He is with me whenever I need Him.** (Page 45)

■   Read Acts 17:27 and James 4:8. Emphasize that there is a difference between God being near to us and us being near to God. God's **omnipresence** means that He is always near to us no matter where we may be. *But that does not mean we are always near to Him.* It's like the old saying, "If God seems far away, guess who moved?" The answer will always be -- you moved, because God is always near to us.

■   Ask your students to suggest practical ways in which they can draw near to God this week.

APPLICATION:

■ Hebrews 13:5-6 offers a fitting summary to the lesson. In it, God says to His people, "I will never leave you." This is the heart of what **omnipresence** is all about.

■ Here's a simple way to remember that: Hold up your hand with palm open and fingers extended. There are five words in the phrase, "I will never leave you." As you say the phrase slowly, bend one of your fingers for each of the words. Do it again, only a bit faster. Then have your students join you. There may be a few smiles and some good-natured groans but encourage everyone to join in. Remind them that this is more than just a game. This is what God's **omnipresence** actually means to them.

■ When they have said the phrase, their fingers will be tightly closed in a ball, like a fist. That fist is like the Lord holding our hand -- just like He said He would in Psalm 37.

■ **Project:** If you wish, you can distribute 3 X 5 cards with the following phrase in bold print: **MY GOD IS BIG ENOUGH TO . . .** Encourage the students to write down one area of their life they believe God is big enough to help them with this week. Tell them to keep the card as a reminder that God is always ready to help them whenever they call on Him.

PRAYER:

"Thank you, Lord, that no matter where we go this week, You will already be there. Thank you for never leaving us even in the hardest of hard times. Amen."

YOUR GOD MUST BE IN CONTROL

RELATES TO STUDENT MANUAL PAGES 47-56

INTRODUCTION:

There are several things to think about in preparation for teaching this chapter. The doctrine of the **sovereignty** of God is one that Christians have expressed in different ways across the centuries. There is agreement on the central fact -- that God is **sovereign** over the affairs of the universe --and some diversity of opinion over how the **sovereignty** of God relates to the freewill of man. Before teaching this chapter, it would be helpful to read your church's statement of faith carefully to see how it handles this issue. You also might discuss this chapter with your pastor in order to get his point of view.

The outline of the chapter is very simple. There are two points that explain what **sovereignty** does mean, and one that clarifies what it does not mean. Be sure to leave at least half of your lesson time to cover the third point. It is nearly as long as the first two put together and provides a very crucial clarification.

HOOK:

Begin this lesson by writing the word **"FREEDOM"** on the board or the overhead in very large, very bold letters. Then say, "There's a lot of talk about what this word really means. How would you define it?" Write down the various answers without comment or interpretation.

Most of the answers will end up something like this: "Freedom is the right to do whatever I want to do whenever I want to do it." Such a definition might be called "Absolute freedom." Ask your students if anyone in the world has absolute freedom. After some discussion, they will conclude that the answer is no. Why not? 1. Because what you want to do may conflict with what I want to do. As the old saying goes, your right to swing your fist ends where my nose begins! 2. Because what you want to do may conflict with the laws of nature. You can flap your arms all day long, but you still won't be able to fly.

The point is, no matter how much we talk about it, no one is completely free. But what about God? Is He free? The answer is yes. God is free because He is **sovereign**. Write that last sentence on the overhead along with the definition from page 47: *God's sovereignty is His absolute control over all that exists and over all that takes place everywhere.*

KEY PRINCIPLES FROM CHAPTER FIVE:

1. *GOD'S SOVEREIGNTY MEANS THAT HE ALONE ALWAYS HAS THE FREEDOM TO DO WHATEVER HE CHOOSES.*

2. *GOD'S SOVEREIGNTY MEANS THAT NO ONE CAN OVERRULE HIM.*

3. *GOD'S SOVEREIGNTY DOES NOT MEAN THAT HIS WILL IS ALWAYS DONE ON EARTH.*

Key Principle # 1: GOD'S SOVEREIGNTY MEANS THAT HE ALONE ALWAYS HAS THE FREEDOM TO DO WHATEVER HE CHOOSES.

■ Read Psalm 115:2-3 and complete the three questions on page 48. You might even do an "IF I WERE GOD" PROJECT. Simply say, "Let's suppose that for one day you had the type of freedom God has. That is, for one day you were the ruler of the universe and you could do and say anything you wanted. You could simply speak a word and it would happen. What would be the first thing you would do? The first thing you would say? The first thing you would change in the universe?" The answers you get from this project will range from the frivolous ("I would make a banana split bigger than Mt. Everest and then I would eat it") to the personal ("I would make it so I didn't have to wear glasses anymore") to the very serious ("I would make all the sick people get well"). The careful teacher can use this project to gain valuable insight into his students. This will also point out that it's good that only God is truly **sovereign** because the rest of us could never agree on what should be done.

■ The paragraph at the bottom of page 48 is a very strong statement about the sovereignty of God. **Do not read it until your students have wrestled with the preceding three questions.** After all, there may be some students who think it is "bad news" that God does "whatever He pleases." But remind your students that God is not like a cosmic computer spitting out random numbers and decisions. *God's sovereignty means that He has perfect freedom to carry out His perfect plan.* Since God's plan is always wise and good and in our own best interest, the truth about His sovereignty is a comfort, not a burden.

Key Principle # 2: GOD'S SOVEREIGNTY MEANS THAT NO ONE CAN OVERRULE HIM.

■ This section should not take too much time since it functions as a bridge to the third principle. The great problem with teaching God's **sovereignty** is that the more you stress the fact that God is in control, the more it appears that He is **not** in control. That is, everywhere evil men grow bolder and bolder. How does that self-evident fact square with God's **sovereignty**?

- This section offers one part of the answer. No matter how messed up the world may appear, God is still in control and no one can overrule Him.

- If you are pressed for time, focus on the quotation from Isaiah 40:15,17 on page 50. Lead your students through the three questions at the bottom of that page and then read the paragraph at the top of page 52.

- Point out how God views things from His perspective:

    The nations are like:
    Drops in a bucket
    Specks of dust on the scales (Isaiah 40:15)

    The inhabitants are like:
    Grasshoppers (Isaiah 40:22)

Key Principle # 3: GOD'S SOVEREIGNTY DOES NOT MEAN HIS WILL IS ALWAYS DONE ON EARTH.

- This is the key section of the chapter. "If God is in control, why is the world in such a mess?" This is **the** great question about God's **sovereignty**.

- This section offers two basic answers to that question:

    1. God has given men the option to obey or disobey His will.

    2. Men everywhere have chosen to disobey God.

- Spend some time lecturing on Deuteronomy 30:17-20. Note the words of Moses: "I have set before you life and death. . . . So choose life." Point out that each of us faces that same choice. Death and suffering come to those who choose to disobey God; life and happiness come to those who choose to obey Him. The issue is the *choice* each one of us must make.

- Make a "Life and Death" chart and ask your students to help you fill it out. Explain that "life" in this context is more than just physical existence. It is the "abundant life" of joy and fulfillment. "Death" is more than just physical death. It is suffering and frustration and lack of fulfillment. Make two columns and ask for examples of:

Choices that lead to Life	Choices that lead to Death
Reading the Bible	*Drug abuse, Alcohol abuse*
Doing homework	*Skipping school*
Dating other Christians	*Premarital sex*
Kindness toward parents	*Bitterness toward parents*

■ If you do this project, it would be good to let both lists get quite long. By doing that, you make it plain that the *choice* each one of us must make is actually a series of daily *choices*. Life and death are set before each of us every single day. Part of God's **sovereignty** is that He gives us the freedom to make those *choices* for ourselves and then to live with the (good or bad) *consequences*.

■ The chapter closes by examining one other aspect of God's **sovereignty**. What about those bad things that happen to us which we don't deserve? That is, what about earthquakes and accidents and sickness? What about the young people who die driving home from church when they are hit by a drunk driver? How does a tragedy like that square with the **sovereignty** of God?

■ The material on page 55 offers the basic outline for answering that question. You may wish to lecture through the material or handle it by asking the students to complete the questions in small groups. The point is, the tragedies that happen are truly tragedies. God's **sovereignty** does not turn bad things into good things. But it does mean that behind the tragedy God has a good and loving purpose. We may not always see it or understand it, but it is there nonetheless.

■ TESTIMONY: An ideal way to handle this difficult issue would be to ask someone who has gone through a tragedy to share a testimony with your students. Ask the person giving the testimony to share not only the difficulty, but also how God brought them through it and what they have learned from it. Such a testimony would be an incredibly powerful way to drive home the point that God is at work even in the darkest moments of life.

■ Another possibility is to arrange for a showing of **When Tragedy Strikes**, a 45-minute video featuring Dawson McAllister and the testimonies of numerous teenagers who survived two terrible bus accidents. The video is available from Shepherd Ministries.

■ The first two paragraphs on page 56 offer an excellent summary of the entire chapter. The teacher should read those paragraphs and then ask the students to read the quotation from Daniel 4:34-35 in unison.

APPLICATION

■ Remind your students that God's **sovereignty** isn't just a theological doctrine. It's the most basic truth in the universe. As the manual says, He is Boss! That means He deserves our daily obedience.

■ Go back to the "Life and Death" chart and remind your students that each day we make a whole series of *choices* that lead to life or to death.

■ Challenge your students to choose one of the "Life" choices this week. Have a time of silent prayer in which they can ask God's help to make that choice this week.

■ Close by singing an appropriate chorus such as "Lord I Will."

PRAYER:

"Thank you, Lord, for being in control of even the tiniest details of life. Amen."

YOUR GOD MUST BE HOLY

RELATES TO STUDENT MANUAL PAGES 57-65

INTRODUCTION:

With this lesson, we turn a corner in our study of God's attributes. The last four lessons have discussed aspects of God's nature which make Him completely different from us:

OMNIPOTENCE: "YOUR GOD MUST BE STRONG"   Chapter 2
OMNISCIENCE: "YOUR GOD MUST KNOW EVERYTHING"   Chapter 3
OMNIPRESENCE: "YOUR GOD MUST BE BIG"   Chapter 4
SOVEREIGNTY: "YOUR GOD MUST BE IN CONTROL"   Chapter 5

Beginning with lesson 6, the manual focuses on various aspects of God's character. What is He like? How does He relate to us? How can we be like Him?

That last question brings out an essential difference. The next four chapters discuss aspects of God's character that we as His children may reflect in our daily living:

The wise teacher will find that these chapters offer a wealth of applicational material. In each case, you can make a direct bridge from the character of God to the character of your students, e.g., "God is _____, therefore we ought to be _____."

HOOK:

Write the following four words on the overhead or blackboard:

Loving

Holy

Trustworthy

Joyful

Ask your students to think carefully and then decide which one of these character qualities they would most like to be true of their lives. Don't discuss or define the words in any way; just let the students make their choice. Then make a tally of how many choose each quality. The results may surprise you and may spark an interesting discussion.

Then ask the question found on page 57: "Would you consider it a compliment if someone called you a holy person? Why or why not?" Let the students discuss the question briefly and then ask, "How many of you would call yourself a holy person?"

The truth is, most of us would have mixed feelings if someone called us a holy person. It all depends on whom is talking! To be called holy could be compliment or an insult.

It's that same uncertainty that makes most of us unwilling to call ourselves holy. We would be more likely to call ourselves loving or trustworthy or joyful.

Holiness makes us uneasy because we're not sure what it means. We know from the Bible though that it is a basic description of God's character.

KEY PRINCIPLES FROM CHAPTER SIX:

---

1.   GOD IS SO HOLY THAT HE IS SEPARATED FROM ALL EVIL.

2.   GOD IS SO HOLY THAT HE CAN NEITHER SIN NOR BE TEMPTED TO SIN.

3.   GOD IS SO HOLY THAT HE HATES SIN.

4.   GOD IS SO HOLY THAT ONE DAY HE WILL WIPE OUT SIN AND ITS CONSEQUENCES.

Key Principle # 1: **GOD IS SO HOLY THAT HE IS SEPARATED FROM ALL EVIL.**

■ The key to this chapter is the definition at the bottom of page 57: "To say that God is holy means that he possesses absolute moral purity and separation from all that is evil."

■ The key word in that definition is "separation." God by His very nature is infinitely separated from all that is evil. This is the concept that must be communicated to your students.

■ **Role Play**: Here's a simple way to stress the concept of separation. Ask one student to play the role of God and another to play the role of "Mr. Evil." At first "God" and "Mr. Evil" stand face to face. "Mr. Evil" calls out a sin (e.g., "Pride") and "God" says, "You cannot come near me." At the same time "God" takes a step backward. "Mr. Evil" calls out another sin ("Anger") and "God" says, "You cannot come near me," taking another step backward. And so it goes a third time and a fourth and a fifth until "Mr. Evil" and "God" are separated by as much space as your room will allow. If in the end they separated by 50 feet and "God" is out the door and down the hall, so much the better. The point is, God will not and cannot coexist with evil.

■ Having done the role play, the teacher should explain the meaning of Isaiah 57:15. The manual makes the helpful point that while God is separated from sin forever, that does not mean he is forever separated from sinners. God draws near to those who mourn over their sin and come to Him for forgiveness.

■ *Holiness means, then, that God has nothing in common with evil. He is in a class by Himself, infinitely above the best that man could produce.*

Key Principle # 2: GOD IS SO HOLY THAT HE CAN NEITHER SIN NOR BE TEMPTED TO SIN.

■ This section builds on the previous one. The key is the thought expressed in I John 1:5 -- "God is light." Stress to your students that light and darkness are opposites. When light enters a room, darkness must leave.

■ There is a fairly simple way to illustrate this concept. Turn off the light and teach in the darkness for a few minutes. The closer to total darkness, the better. Keep the lights off long enough so that your eyes can adjust to the change. Then, on a prearranged signal, have the lights turned on again. The sudden change will leave your students (and you) blinking their eyes. But that's the crucial point: God is light, and where light is, darkness must leave.

■ Take time to complete the "GOD IS LIGHT" PROJECT on page 60.

■ Summarize the implications of James 1:13 for your students. This is the "bottom line" on God's **holiness**. As a project, you want to print this verse on a small card and encourage your students to memorize it during the week.

Key Principle # 3: GOD IS SO HOLY THAT HE HATES SIN.

■ **Teacher's note**: You might notice the progression of thought in this lesson:

Principle # 1: God is forever separated from sin
Principle # 2: God has no fellowship with sin
Principle # 3: God hates sin

■ Stress to your students that they will never understand God's **holiness** until they grasp how God views sin. And they will never become holy until they begin to view sin the way God does.

■ The key in teaching this section is to capitalize upon the surprise factor. As the manual notes, many people are surprised to learn that God hates anything.

■ Make a chart entitled "Seven Things God Hates" from Proverbs 6:16-19. List the seven sins on the left and ask your students to give contemporary examples of each sin. The ideal would be to have three or four examples for each sin listed.

■ At this time the teacher must press home the point made on page 62: -- How quickly and how easily and how glibly and how thoughtlessly we repeatedly do the things that God hates. That is, we -- whom God loves -- often do the things which God hates. *The point must be stressed that even though God loves us, His holiness compels Him to hate the sin we so carelessly commit!*

Key Principle # 4: GOD IS SO HOLY THAT ONE DAY HE WILL WIPE OUT SIN AND ITS CONSEQUENCES.

■ This entire section is keyed to the Scripture from II Peter 3. The key question is the one at the top of page 64 -- Why will God one day burn up the earth and all that is in it? That is, after all that God did to create the world, why will He one day burn it up? Allow time for your students to offer several possible answers to that question.

■ Point out that the answer has to do with God's **holiness**. He hates sin so much that He will one day destroy the present universe and replace it with one in which there is no sin. This is the logical climax of the entire chapter:

> God is separated from sin
> God has no fellowship with sin
> God hates sin
> God will one day wipe out sin and its consequences

APPLICATION:

■ Go back to the question from the introduction: "Would you consider it a compliment if someone called you a holy person?" Ask the students how they would answer that question in light of this lesson.

■ Then ask, "Would you call yourself a holy person? Why or why not?"

■ Then ask, "What would have to change in your life before you would be truly holy?" Urge your students to be honest with themselves.

■ Point out that **holiness** is only possible when we finally see our sin the way God sees it and when we hate it as He hates it. Anything less -- tolerating or excusing our sinfulness -- is simply not **holiness**.

■ The good news is the quotation from Isaiah 57:15 -- The Most High God draws near to the contrite and lowly in spirit.

■ Have your students pray silently, talking to God about the things that would have to change before they would be truly holy.

PRAYER:

"Holy Father, open our eyes that we might truly see You, and having seen You, to see ourselves as You see us. Amen."

YOUR GOD MUST BE LOVING

RELATES TO STUDENT MANUAL PAGES 67-76

INTRODUCTION:

This particular lesson probably will be one of the more enjoyable ones in the series. As the manual notes, most people know that God is love. That means you probably won't have to spend time trying to prove the point to your students.

The real challenge of this lesson is in communicating the greatness of God's love. The manual uses words like "infinite," "vast," and "everlasting." The various projects and illustrations are meant as tools to help you bridge the gap between the very imperfect love your students experience and the love of God which those words express.

Several references are made to the use of music. The suggestions which are made are intended only to point you in the right direction. With a little forethought -- and without too much extra effort -- you should be able to find suitable secular music which speaks of the universal desire for love and suitable Christian music which speaks of God's love. In this area, you are limited only by your time and creativity.

The bottom line: You probably will greatly enjoy teaching this lesson, but don't take it for granted. The extra time you spend in preparation will be well worth the effort.

HOOK:

- Write the word **LOVE** in enormous letters on the overhead or blackboard.

- As the class is getting ready to start, play the old pop song "What the World Needs Now" in the background.

- Begin by asking your class to give you the names of popular songs with the word "Love" in the title. You'll probably need a couple of examples to help them get started. Don't worry about the message of the songs. You aren't going to do music analysis. Just write down the titles on the overhead or blackboard.

- Point out that everyone is interested in love. The need to be loved is one of the universal needs of mankind. That is why there is no end to songs (and books and movies) on this topic.

- Two of the songs' lyrics point out the dilemma of this generation: "What the world needs now is love, sweet love," but people are "looking for love in all the wrong places."

- The good news is, they don't have to look any farther than the Bible because the Bible reveals that God is love. What the world needs and what people are looking for is the love which ultimately comes from God alone.

- From that beginning, point out the definition of God's love on page 67: *God's love is His intense desire and commitment to shower deep affection and complete self-sacrifice upon all mankind.*

KEY PRINCIPLES FROM CHAPTER SEVEN:

---

1. *GOD IS SO LOVING, BECAUSE ALL LOVE ORIGINATES FROM HIM.*

2. *GOD IS SO LOVING, BECAUSE HIS LOVE IS EVERLASTING AND LIMITLESS.*

3. *GOD IS SO LOVING, BECAUSE HIS LOVE IS SACRIFICIAL AND LOYAL.*

4. *GOD'S LOVE MOTIVATES US TO LOVE HIM AND OTHERS.*

Key Principle # 1: **GOD IS SO LOVING, BECAUSE ALL LOVE ORIGINATES FROM HIM.**

■ There are really only two things you need to do to teach this section. First, read I John 4:7-8 and explain the meaning of the phrase "for love is from God." He is the <u>source</u> of all the love in the universe. It <u>flows</u> from Him like a river flows from a spring hidden beneath the earth.

■ Second, point out that since God is the source of all the love in the universe, every act of human love has its ultimate source in Him. That is, even when people who deny God's existence perform an act of love toward someone else, they are giving an unconscious testimony to God because "love is of God." Without God, there would no love, no kindness, no generosity, no affection anywhere in the universe.

■ To drive this home, have your students complete the "GOD'S LOVE IN THE WORLD" PROJECT on page 68. Point out that these things are done by believers and unbelievers alike, that love is found in every race and culture and nation, that love knows no boundaries. It is the universal language. Love may be found everywhere because God may be found everywhere. cf. Lesson 4, "YOUR GOD MUST BE BIG."

Key Principle # 2: GOD IS SO LOVING, BECAUSE HIS LOVE IS EVERLASTING AND LIMITLESS.

■ **The "How Many People Do You Love" Project.** Ask your students to write on a piece of paper the number of people they love right now. Tell them not to worry about the definition of love or the fact that they love different people in different ways. Just tell them to write down their best guess. Collect the numbers and write them down one by one on one side of the overhead or blackboard. Label that side "Our Love" and make a total at the bottom. Label the other side "God's Love" and write 5,000,000,000 at the bottom. No matter how big the number is on the left side, it pales against the number on the right side. God's love is greater!

■ Point out from Psalm 103:17 that God's love is "from everlasting to everlasting." That means it started before time began and will last after time finally runs out. It has no beginning and it has no ending.

■ Take time to complete the questions from Romans 8:38-39 on page 71. The wonderful thing about this passage is the long list of things that <u>cannot</u> separate us from God's love. Tell your students it's like the children's game Red Rover. In that game, teammates join hands and call for a member from the opposing team to try to run through their joined hands. If he makes it through, he takes a person back with him to the other team. If he can't break through, he had to join that team. Paul is saying that God's love has joined hands with us and no one and nothing can ever break through. Not even death can break through because we are joined forever with the love of God. Not even the Devil and all his infernal power can break through because God's love is holding us tight.

Key Principle # 3: GOD IS SO LOVING, BECAUSE HIS LOVE IS SACRIFICIAL AND LOYAL.

■ This principle comes to the heart of God's love. Ask your students, "If you genuinely love someone, what is the greatest thing you could ever do

41

for them?" The answer is found in John 15:13 -- you lay down your life for your friends.

■ Then ask your students, How many people would you be willing to die for? This is the final question on page 73. Give them time to write down the names and the reason that they would die. This is a solemn question and if done correctly, will engage your students in some deep thinking.

■ At this point, lecture on Romans 5:6-8. The point to bring out is the contrast between verse 7 and verse 8. Paul emphasizes that the only kind of person most of us would die for would be a righteous person -- someone we highly respected for the quality of his life. Even then, many of us wouldn't do that. Stress the first two words of verse 8 -- **"But God"**. In those two words is the heart of the Gospel. God did what we would never do. He sent His Son to die -- not for righteous men, but for sinners.

■ Stress that there is a difference between talking about love and doing something about it. When Romans 5:8 says God "demonstrated" His love, it means He did more than just talk about it. He sent His Son as a practical, visible demonstration of His love for us.

■ Pages 74-75 introduce us to a second aspect of God's love. It is **loyal love**. Have your students read Psalm 139:17-18 and stress that God is thinking loving thoughts of them right now!

■ **The "Note To God" Project**. At the top of page 75 there is space for your students to write a note to God. This is probably best done in groups of 3 or 4 people. Give your students 5 minutes to compose a brief note to God. Have each group read its note out loud to the class.

Key Principle # 4: GOD'S LOVE MOTIVATES US TO LOVE HIM AND OTHERS.

■ **Teacher's Note**: It will be helpful to tie this section in with the first section about all love finding its source in God. Remind your students that every expression of human love -- no matter how imperfect -- finds its source in God because "love is from God." There is no love without God.

■ Remind your students that the ultimate evidence that we belong to God is that we love our brothers and sisters -- John 13:34-35. It is the ultimate evidence because love is something everyone understands.

■ Replay the song "What The World Needs Now."

■ Complete the "LOVING WITH GOD'S LOVE" PROJECT on pages 75-76.

APPLICATION:

■ Give your students a "Biblical Love Analysis." Use the characteristics of God's love printed on page 76 as your basis. Type the 11 characteristics on the left side of a sheet of paper with the numbers:
1   2   3   4 beside each one. The key is as follows:

    1 = I am very weak in this area

    2 = I am neither weak nor strong in this area

    3 = I am getting stronger in this area

    4 = I am strong in this area

■ Give them a few minutes to complete the test with the encouragement that they should be as honest as possible -- both about their strengths and their weaknesses.

■ After everyone is finished, ask the students to notice which areas they circled with either a 1 or a 2.

■ Ask them to pick out one of those areas to pray about this week.

■ Remind your students that since all love comes from God, when they ask Him to help them be more loving, they can be sure that He will always answer that prayer.

■ **Teaching Aid**: As means of driving the lesson home, give each student a sticker which reads "God loves you." These are available at any Christian bookstore or you could make your own stickers. Encourage your students to put their sticker where they can see it each day. "Let it be a reminder to pray for God's love to be evident in your life."

PRAYER:

"Lord Jesus, you showed us what love was all about when you died for us. Help us to walk in your love this week. Amen."

YOUR GOD MUST BE MERCIFUL AND GRACIOUS

RELATES TO STUDENT MANUAL PAGES 77-86

INTRODUCTION:

The challenge in teaching this lesson is that you are dealing with two similar -- but not identical -- attributes of God. Mercy and Grace are not the same thing, though they are clearly related. Very simplified:

- Mercy means God withholds punishment from those who deserve it.
- Grace means God gives eternal life to those who don't deserve it.

In your teaching, point out that mercy and grace are like two sides of a coin -- they go together. We are the recipients of both the mercy **and** the grace of God.

The mood and tone of this lesson ought to be upbeat and encouraging. God's mercy is good news; His grace is even better news. Make sure your students catch that spirit as you teach this lesson.

HOOK:

Divide your students into several small groups and give each group all three statements written on a piece of paper. Ask each group to "Tell Us About" all three statements.

1. Tell us about a time when you were punished for something you didn't do.

2. Tell us about a time when you did something wrong and were not punished for it even though you knew you should have been.

3. Tell us about a time when you had someone give you a nice gift (or award or honor) and you almost felt embarrassed because you knew you didn't deserve it.

It should be easy to get plenty of response because all three statements describe common human situations -- being punished wrongly, not being punished when we ought to be, being given something we don't deserve.

There are two attributes of God which explore what we deserve and don't deserve from God's point of view. Those two attributes are **Mercy** and **Grace**.

KEY PRINCIPLES FROM CHAPTER EIGHT:

---

*1.   GOD IS MERCIFUL TO ALL HIS CREATURES,
       EVEN THE UNGRATEFUL.*

*2.   GOD IS GRACIOUS TO ALL HIS CREATURES,
       BECAUSE MAN IS UTTERLY HELPLESS TO SAVE
       HIMSELF.*

*3.   GOD'S GRACE IS A FREE AND UNDESERVED
       GIFT.*

*4.   GOD'S MERCY AND GRACE MOTIVATE US TO
       GIVE OUR WHOLE LIFE TO HIM.*

Key Principle # 1: **GOD IS MERCIFUL TO ALL HIS CREATURES, EVEN THE UNGRATEFUL.**

■ There are three parts to this section and each one adds something important to our knowledge of God's mercy.

■ The quotation from Psalm 145:8-9 (page 78) is meant to show that "God's mercy is not limited to God's people." After reading this passage, ask your students to name some ways in which even <u>unbelievers</u> experience the mercy of God. Then ask, what would happen to this world if even for one day God allowed mankind to experience the full effect of sin?

■ A useful Scripture to use in this regard is II Peter 3:9 which speaks of God withholding the final judgment in order that men may have more time to repent of their sins.

■ The quotation from Psalm 145:14-19 (page 79) is meant to show that "God reaches out in mercy to help and comfort those who are in distress."

■ **The "Hunger and Thirst" Project**. Here is an interesting twist on this passage. Psalm 145 says that God constantly satisfies the hunger and thirst of every living thing. Yet we know that there are many people around the world who go to bed hungry every night. How does that square with what Psalm 145 says? Is God merciful or isn't He? Let your students wrestle with that one for awhile.

The answer to that dilemma must lie along the following lines. God is merciful and His mercy is seen all around us. His mercy includes creating rich farmland and sending rain to water the fields. But fields do not harvest themselves. Part of God's mercy is seen in the men and women who harvest, transport, and prepare the food. They are <u>agents</u> of God's mercy. If millions are people are hungry tonight, is it not because all of us have been too concerned about ourselves and too little concerned about others? The great challenge to us who are the <u>recipients</u> of God's mercy is to become the <u>agents</u> of God's mercy in our daily lives. That certainly includes caring about those who have less than we do.

(This project is included at this point in the lesson, but could be used as the application at the end, if so desired. In that case, simply add an opportunity for your students to contribute to a Christian relief project --such as the World Vision "Love Loaf" campaign.)

■ The "GOD IS MERCIFUL TO ALL" PROJECT on page 80 is meant to show that God is merciful even to people who do not appreciate His mercy. If you do this project, it would be good to complete it on an overhead as the students give you their answers.

<u>Key Principle # 2</u>: GOD IS GRACIOUS TO ALL HIS CREATURES, BECAUSE MAN IS UTTERLY HELPLESS TO SAVE HIMSELF.

■ This is a good place to point out the difference between mercy and grace. Mercy means God <u>withholds</u> punishment. Grace means God gives the <u>undeserved</u> gift of eternal life. To say it another way, **mercy** means you *don't* get what you *do* deserve, while **grace** means you *do* get what you *don't* deserve.

■ This section is meant to prove only the last part of that statement -- we **don't** deserve eternal life. Ephesians 2:1-3 gives us three sources for our evil behavior:

1. The crowd (The world)
2. Satan (The devil)
3. Our evil natures (The flesh)

■ In explaining this passage, spend time on the first and last statements:

"You were under God's curse, doomed forever for your sins."
"We started out bad . . . and were under God's anger."

■ Suppose we could take 100 men and women off the street and read them this passage. How would they react to it? Which parts of it would be hardest for them to accept? Why?

■ Someone has said that the grace of God is the hardest doctrine of all for man to accept. Why?

■ Ask your students to suppose that two teenagers die and suddenly stand side-by-side before God. One was raised in the church, never missed Sunday School, read his Bible every day, and witnessed to his friends at school. The other dropped out of church when he was a little kid, started dealing dope when he was 14, robbed a liquor store when he was 15, and shot a man when he was 16. By coincidence they both died at the same time. Which of these two teenagers is in greater need of the grace of God? (Answer: They both stand in desperate need of God's grace. The fact that one teenager appears more righteous than the other does not change the bottom line. The truth is, going to church does not make a person even a tiny bit more acceptable to God. You should stress this fact lest your students unconsciously assume that they don't really need God's grace.)

Key Principle # 3: GOD'S GRACE IS A FREE AND UNDESERVED GIFT.

■ This section is essentially a continuation of the previous one, so there should be very little break in your teaching.

■ The most interesting question is the one posed at the top of page 83 -- "Why do you think it is impossible for a person's good deeds to get him to heaven?" Let your students suggest as many answers as possible, i.e., "No one can ever do enough good deeds," "You never know which ones count the most," "Your sins cancel out your good deeds."

■ **Illustration**: Tell your students that you are going to give a dollar as a gift to anyone who wants it. Tell them all they have to do is come up front and get it. (You'll probably have to offer it more than once.) When someone comes up and asks for the dollar, tell them you'll give it to them as a free gift if they will do 50 pushups. When they object, tell them it's a free gift as long as they do the 50 pushups in front of the whole group. Eventually, someone will point out that it's not a free gift if you have to do 50 pushups to get the dollar. Then you say, "That's right! A free gift means you don't have to do anything to get it." Then say to the person who came forward, "Do you still want the dollar? This time it's really a free gift." Then give the dollar to them.

■ Point out Romans 11:6 and drive home the fact that grace and works are opposites. As long as you are trying (or hoping) to work your way to heaven, you aren't depending upon God's grace. But when you stop working and start trusting, then God's grace saves you. *"God's forgiveness is a free and undeserved gift from God and is not prompted by anything we do."* (page 83)

Key Principle # 4: GOD'S MERCY AND GRACE MOTIVATE US TO GIVE OUR WHOLE LIFE TO HIM.

■ This final section is a logical climax to the whole lesson. It is based on Romans 12:1, a very familiar passage.

■ Lecture briefly about the Old Testament background of the phrase "living sacrifice." Point out that God required the Israelites to offer animals as sacrifices. As the manual points out, "a sacrifice is something that we give up." The Israelites gave up (offered) their animals to God as a sign of their devotion to Him. There were two major differences between the Old Testament sacrifices and the "living sacrifice" of Romans 12:1. First, in the Old Testament the believers offers animals to God; in the New Testament believers offer themselves to God. Second, in the Old Testament the animals were killed and then offered; in the New Testament believers offer themselves while they are still alive.

■ The point is, God doesn't want animals offered to Him anymore. He wants His people to offer themselves. And he doesn't want any more blood shed. The blood of His Son is fully sufficient.

■ But why does God want us to offer our <u>bodies</u>? Because if He has our bodies, He's got us! We can't go anywhere without our bodies.

■ Therefore, the logical and proper response to the mercies of God is to present our bodies to God -- as a sign of our devotion to Him.

APPLICATION:

■ The "LIVING SACRIFICE" PROJECT on page 84 would be an excellent way to end this lesson. Make sure you have enough time left so you don't rush through this project. Encourage your students to write their prayers in the space provided.

■ Close by singing the chorus "In My Life, Lord, Be Glorified." Sing it through once for each part of the body mentioned in the project, i.e., "With my tongue, Lord, be glorified."

PRAYER:

"Lord, thank you for giving us less than what we really deserve and far more than we could ever earn. Amen."

YOUR GOD MUST BE TRUSTWORTHY

RELATES TO STUDENT MANUAL PAGES 88-98

INTRODUCTION:

Your aim is this lesson is delightfully simple: To convince your students that God is indeed trustworthy. The challenge is the one mentioned on page 89: "God, unlike the world around us, is trustworthy." That is the key to teaching this lesson. The three points made about God are untrue of the world around us:

1. The world is not eternal, and nothing in the world is eternal.
2. Everything in this world changes constantly.
3. There is no one who always does what he says.

Against the backdrop of an ever-changing, non-eternal world where people regularly break their word stands the trustworthiness of God. It will help to remember as you teach this lesson that many of your students need to hear this lesson precisely because the world they live in is so unreliable. For some teenagers, God may be the only trustworthy person they know.

HOOK:

Here is an idea that has been around for awhile, but is still very effective. Clear the chairs away and have your students pair off. One student stands with his back to the other student. The other student stands two feet away. On a signal, the partner in front falls backward, keeping his body taut. The student in back must catch his falling partner. Do it once or twice and then have the students switch places.

Inevitably, some students simply will refuse to do this. Others will go through with it, but reluctantly. A few will do it easily.

After the exercise is over, have the students sit down and then ask these questions:

1. How did you feel when you began to fall backwards?

2. Was it harder to do the falling or the catching?

3. Why is this exercise scary for most people?

It's the answer to the last one that is the key. It's scary because the person in front has to trust the person in back -- whom they know but cannot see. *Trust is hard because you never know what the other person is going to do.*

Point out that we live in a world which makes it difficult to trust other people -- even people we know very well. That's the bad news. The good news is that there is one Person we can trust completely -- God. He is **Trustworthy**.

KEY PRINCIPLES FROM CHAPTER NINE:

---

1.   *GOD IS TRUSTWORTHY, BECAUSE HE IS ETERNAL.*

2.   *GOD IS TRUSTWORTHY, BECAUSE HE NEVER CHANGES.*

3.   *GOD IS TRUSTWORTHY, BECAUSE HE ALWAYS DOES WHAT HE SAYS.*

Key Principle # 1: GOD IS TRUSTWORTHY, BECAUSE HE IS ETERNAL.

■   The concept of eternity is difficult to grasp. Something which is eternal has no beginning and it has no ending. It always is. Psalm 90 tells us that although the world is not eternal, God is. He is "from everlasting to everlasting." That means that if you got in a time capsule and went back, back, back, back, back into the farthest reaches of the distant past, back to the creation of the universe -- God would still be there. And if you went to the end of time, millions and billions of years into the future, God would still be there.

■   **The "Things Which are Eternal" Project**. Make a chart on the overhead with a line drawn down the middle. Label the left side "Eternal" and the right side "Not Eternal." Let your students help you fill it out. On the right side, list such things as "The Himalayas," "The Pacific Ocean," "Sit-coms," "'57 Chevies," "Atom bombs," "Zits," "Peewee Herman." It doesn't really matter how long the right list is. Be sure to add "Sin," "Satan," and "Death" to the right hand list. Only one name should be listed on the left side of the chart -- "God."

(Someone may ask if people should be listed as eternal. The answer is no, because something which is eternal has no beginning. All of us had our beginning in our mother's womb. There was a moment when we were not, and then a moment when we began our lives. So we are not eternal in the sense that God is.)

■ Now go to page 90 and complete the questions on II Peter 3:8. Stress that because God is eternal, He is not limited by time as we are. He stands outside of time, viewing it from above as you would view a parade from the 45th floor of a skyscraper. We are like the people who sit in the reviewing stand watching each float go by one by one. But God sees the whole parade from beginning to end. Time to us goes by so slowly. But not to God.

■ Point out the practical value of this truth. Since yesterday, today and tomorrow are the same to Him, nothing that happens to us catches Him off guard. The things which surprise us do not surprise Him at all. He sees how everything fits into His master plan for us.

■ Finally, point out the implications of Psalm 102. First, it clearly teaches that this universe will one day come to an end. Second, it clearly teaches that God will remain even after the universe perishes. (If you wish, you can relate this back to the discussion of II Peter 3:10-13 on pages 62-64.)

Key Principle # 2: GOD IS TRUSTWORTHY, BECAUSE HE NEVER CHANGES.

■ Lecture on the material on pages 93-94. The essential point to make is that God's character never changes. He was holy in the past; He is holy today. He possessed all wisdom from the beginning and He possesses all wisdom today. God has never "learned" anything because He knew it all from the start! Point out that God's changelessness means that He is completely reliable. We can trust Him no matter how our life changes because He never changes.

■ THE "WHO AND WHAT SHOULD I TRUST" PROJECT. Although this project is found in the first section (page 92), it also fits well here. Ask your students to think of the people they admire and respect. It certainly should include their parents and good friends, but also can include famous people they don't know personally. Ask your students to estimate how long those "important people" will live.

■ **Illustration**: While your students are completing this project, or immediately afterwards, play a recording of "Dust In The Wind," by the musical group Kansas. It very effectively drives home the point that we are here today and gone tomorrow. Even the most important people die eventually.

■ As a final follow-up, ask your students to write down one more name -- their own. Then ask them to estimate how long they expect to live. Some teenagers may resist doing this project -- a fact which points out its importance. Remind them that they too will die someday.

■ Close this section by reading aloud and in unison the quotation from Psalm 46 on page 95.

Key Principle # 3: GOD IS TRUSTWORTHY, BECAUSE HE ALWAYS DOES WHAT HE SAYS.

■ Ask your students how many people they know who <u>always</u> do exactly what they say. If they say they are going to do something, they <u>always</u> do exactly what they said, exactly when they said they would do it. If they make a promise, they <u>always</u> keep it. When you put enough qualifiers on it, the answer will always be no one.

■ Point out that to say this is not an insult to your parents, your friends, your teachers, or your pastor. It simply means that no human being is perfectly trustworthy. Even the best of us fail to keep our word perfectly.

■ There is someone though who always keeps His word. That person is God. He has always kept His word and He always will.

■ <u>The "People who Trusted in God" Project</u>. Divide your students into two teams. Each team has five minutes to complete the following assignment: List as many Bible characters as you can who trusted in God at some point in their lives. The kicker: List each name <u>and</u> a specific instance when that person trusted in God. For instance, "Noah -- Built an ark," "Abraham -- Offered Isaac," "Sarah -- Believed God for a child," "Peter -- Walked on water." Put a ticking clock on the podium to add a little suspense to the contest.

■ Wrap up the contest by summarizing the material from Hebrews 11:6 on page 97. Point out that from the very beginning God has been seeking men and women who will trust Him. That is, God seeks those who will seek Him. And when He finds such a person, He rewards him greatly.

56

APPLICATION:

■ **"God Is My Rock."** This is a variation on the "GOD IS OUR REFUGE" PROJECT on page 95. It is suggested by Psalm 18:2, "The Lord is my rock, my fortress and my deliverer."

■ Before class, gather a number of medium-sized rocks -- enough for each student to have one. Clean the rocks and then paint "Psalm 18:2" on each one. Be sure to use paint which will not wash off.

■ Introduce the application by reading the first paragraph from the "GOD IS OUR REFUGE" PROJECT on page 95. Then read Psalm 18:2 and remind your students that a rock is a place of refuge and security. It provides a secure foundation <u>and</u> a safe place to hide in the time of trouble. The stronger the rock you stand upon, the safer you are.

■ When David said, "The Lord is my rock," he was applying the truth of God's trustworthiness to his own situation. <u>God is our rock precisely because he is always and entirely trustworthy.</u>

■ Then give each student a rock with "Psalm 18:2" painted on it. Tell them to put the rock in a place where they can see it each day. It will remind them of God's unchanging faithfulness to them.

■ *****Teacher's Note: This particular project will take some extra preparation time. Don't let that fact make you hesitate. Your students will go away from this lesson with a tangible reminder of what you said and some of them will keep their rocks for years to come.**

■ Close by asking three of your students to lead in prayer. Encourage them to pray prayers of thanksgiving for God's faithfulness to us.

PRAYER:

"Thank you, Lord, that although we change constantly, You never do. Amen."

YOUR GOD MUST BE A PERSON

RELATES TO STUDENT MANUAL PAGES 99-108

INTRODUCTION:

With this lesson we take yet another turn in our study of God's attributes. The manual up to this point may be outlined as follows:

Part 1 -- False Views of God	Chapter 1
Part 2 -- God's Nature	Chapters 2-5
Part 3 -- God's Character	Chapters 6-9

The tenth chapter brings us to Part 4 of our study -- Jesus Christ is God. This lesson, and the one to follow, bring us face to face with the person of Jesus Christ. Chapter 10 stresses His deity; chapter 11 calls for a response of faith. In effect, the manual closes with a very strong presentation of the Gospel. You will find many good opportunities to challenge your students to place their faith in Jesus.

HOOK:

Build your whole lesson off the sentence at the bottom of page 99:
"Although many people will acknowledge that Jesus was a great religious leader, many others deny or are ignorant of the fact that He is also God."

Prepare a brief panel discussion on the theme "Who is Jesus Christ?" A week ahead of time ask four of your students to present four different answers to that question:

A.   The Muslim Answer (A great prophet, but not the Son of God.)
B.   The Humanist Answer (A great example, but not the Son of God.)
C.   The Jewish Answer (A great teacher, but not the Son of God.)
D.   The New Age Answer (A highly-advanced spiritual master, but not the Son of God.)

Ask each student to speak for 2-3 minutes representing that point of view. You will no doubt need to provide guidance to help them prepare their talks.

When the four presentations are finished, thank the panel and then tell your students that they have heard four very popular answers to the question, "Who is Jesus Christ?" "In the next few minutes you will hear a fifth answer -- the answer of the Bible."

KEY PRINCIPLES FROM CHAPTER TEN:

---

1.   JESUS CHRIST IS ALL POWERFUL.

2.   JESUS CHRIST IS HOLY.

3.   JESUS CHRIST IS LOVING.

Key Principle # 1: JESUS CHRIST IS ALL POWERFUL.

■ Stress in your opening comments the quotation from Hebrews 1:1-3 (page 99). Point out that since Jesus is called "the exact representation of His nature," we ought to see the various attributes of God clearly demonstrated in His life. That is, if He is indeed God, the Bible should leave no doubt about that fact. And further, if He is indeed God, not only should there be explicit claims to this fact, but the evidence should be abundant.

■ In fact, it would be good to note that the claims for His deity are so clear that those who hold to other views (such as the four mentioned in the panel discussion) must deliberately ignore or misconstrue the unambiguous evidence of the text.

■ In this lesson you will be tracing the evidence for three primary attributes of God in the life of Jesus -- His power, His holiness, and His love. One possibility would be to divide your students into three groups -- a "Power Group," a "Holiness Group," and a "Love Group." Give the groups 10 minutes to find as much evidence as possible in the life of Christ for their particular attribute.

■ In the section on "Jesus Christ is all powerful," lecture on Colossians 1 (pages 100-102). Call attention to the drawing on page 101. Point out that everything that exists is made up of molecules which are themselves made up of atoms which are made up of protons, neutrons and electrons which are themselves made up of even tinier particles. And behind the tiniest particles stands Jesus Christ who holds all things together.

■ Ask for a report from the "Power Group." Write down their answers on the overhead or blackboard. They should come back with an impressive list of miracles. Stress that the greatest miracle of all is the Resurrection. And Jesus had the power to bring Himself back from the dead! Only God could do that!

Key Principle # 2: JESUS CHRIST IS HOLY.

■ It is crucial to begin by reminding your students what holiness means. To say that God is holy is to say that He is absolutely separated from all sin and evil. He hates it and will ultimately destroy it.

■ Read Hebrews 7:26 and stress that He is both unstained by sin and undefiled by sinners. That is, although He was the friend of sinners, He never became like them and never followed in their sinful ways.

■ Ask for a report from the "Holiness Group." This group may have more difficulty so you may want to tell them to look for occasions when Jesus rebuked men for their sin and their hypocrisy. Encourage them to focus on how Jesus responded to the Pharisees. Have them read Matthew 23 along with John 2:13-17. Write their answers on the overhead or blackboard.

■ Some useful questions to ask:

1. Why did Jesus get so upset with the Pharisees?

2. How would you answer someone who said, "It's not very loving to take a whip and throw people out of the Temple?"

3. How does it make you feel to know that Jesus sometimes got very angry with people?

4. If Jesus visited our youth group, what things would make Him glad and what things would make Him angry?

■ Close by stressing that there is no contradiction between Jesus' love and His holiness. His love is always a holy love and His holiness is expressed in anger because of His great love for mankind. (If you truly love someone, you will be angry with them when they recklessly disobey God. If you don't love them, you'll probably just ignore them.)

Key Principle # 4: JESUS CHRIST IS LOVING.

■ Begin by asking the "Love Group" to report. They should have many examples to give you. Write them on the overhead or blackboard.

■ Emphasize that while most people agree that Jesus Christ is loving, many have never understood the greatest demonstration of His love. This is your chance to share the Gospel clearly with your students. Explain that when Christ died, He died as a sacrifice to take away the sins of the world. A sacrifice is someone or something offered in the place of another person. "Christ was a sacrifice because He took our place on the cross." Explain that when Jesus died on the cross:

      1. He took your place
      2. He paid your penalty

■ "As a result, you don't have to die and you don't have to pay the penalty for your sins. Jesus has already done it for you."

■ "The only thing that God asks is that you believe. To believe means to put your trust in, to rely upon, to place your full confidence in someone. To believe in Jesus Christ means that you understand who He is (God's Son) and what He did (died in your place taking your penalty) and that you are trusting Him and Him alone for the forgiveness of your sins."

■ Close this section by playing one of the contemporary versions of "Jesus Loves Me." There are several good ones available at any Christian bookstore.

APPLICATION:

■ Bring the session full circle by referring to the quotation at the bottom of page 99: "Although many people will acknowledge that Jesus was a great religious leader, many others deny or are ignorant of the fact that He is also God."

■ Remind your class of the answers given by the panel members at the beginning of the class. Point out that there is some truth in each answer. Jesus is a great prophet and a great example and a great teacher and He is the only one who can connect us with God. But He is much more. He is God's only-begotten Son from heaven. He is God's incarnate Son who visited planet earth 2,000 years ago to die for the sins of the world. He is the Savior of the world and the Lord of heaven and earth.

■ The problem with the other views is that they focus on only a part of who He is and what He did. But in the case of Jesus, to be partly right is to be completely wrong. If you miss the truth about Jesus, you have missed the most important truth in all the world.

■ Close by stressing the importance of being right about Jesus. *"This is no place to guess and hope you get it right. Make sure the Jesus you believe in is the Jesus of the Bible and make sure you truly believe in Him."*

PRAYER:

"We thank you, Lord, that You have not left us to wonder about who You are. As You have opened our eyes to see You clearly, so open our hearts to love You supremely. Amen."

MAKE UP YOUR MIND!

RELATES TO STUDENT MANUAL PAGES 109-113

INTRODUCTION:

This is the final lesson on the attributes of God. As you will see, it consists of several elements: A review of the previous lessons, a discussion of the introduction to the entire book, and a study of the final chapter in the manual.

The major teaching challenge will be in deciding where to place your emphasis. Some groups may profit from spending the bulk of the time in review; others may need a strong emphasis on the final chapter. There is enough material for you to develop several different lesson plans.

HOOK:

Photocopy the following review and hand it out to your students. Tell them to draw a line from the word or phrase on the left to the correct definition on the right.

WHO ARE YOU, GOD? MATCH-UP

Grace   Deep affection/Complete self-sacrifice

Deity of Jesus   Separated from all that is evil

Love   Present everywhere

Omnipresence   Withholding punishment

Omniscience   Jesus is God

Holy   In control of everything

False Idea   All-powerful

Trustworthy   Knows everything

Sovereign   Cosmic Killjoy

Omnipotence   Completely reliable

Mercy   God gives us what we don't deserve

As you go over the answers, you will have an excellent opportunity to clarify any words or concepts your students don't understand. Be sure to congratulate the students for completing the manual. In truth, they now have a grasp of who God is that is far beyond the average church member.

KEY PRINCIPLES FROM CHAPTER ELEVEN:

> 1. *BUT YOU DO HAVE A GOD . . .*
>
> 2. *JESUS CHRIST, GOD'S SON, DIED IN YOUR PLACE.*
>
> 3. *JESUS CHRIST, GOD'S SON, OFFERS HIS LIFE TO YOU.*
>
> 4. *JESUS CHRIST, GOD'S SON, WAITS FOR YOU TO RECEIVE HIM.*

Key Principle # 1: **BUT YOU DO HAVE A GOD . . .**

■ After finishing the review, make the transition to the lesson by pointing out that the students can now understand in a new way what the introduction (pages 1-2) means when it says, "But you do have a God . . . " Remind them that the first of the Ten Commandments is, "You shall have no other gods before me." This obviously means that there are other "gods" (little "g") in the universe. What is a "god" in that sense? A "god" (or idol) is any object in which you put your ultimate trust. Thus, a "god" could be something which in itself is good -- like education or wealth -- but which becomes an idol because a person places his ultimate trust in it.

■ Make a chart entitled "Everyone has a God." Let the students name some of the modern "gods." Write down the list. It should include some "things" like cars, homes, business empires, and so on. And it also should include some people like rock stars, football heroes, and political and religious leaders. Be sure to point out that these things and people are not wrong in themselves. The crucial issue is the way people look to them for meaning and purpose in life.

■ The third and fourth paragraphs on page 2 are very significant and ought to be read aloud to the students. They stress that each one of us must make a choice. There are "gods" and there is the one true God. "For 10 weeks we have been studying what the Bible says about God. But it is not enough to know the facts about God. We need to know God personally. That's what the final lesson is all about."

Key Principle # 2: JESUS CHRIST, GOD'S SON, DIED IN YOUR PLACE.

■ This section stresses the substitutionary aspect of Christ's death. Spend some time talking about the phrase from I Peter 2:24, "He himself bore our sins in his body on the tree." That's a very literal picture. Stress that crucifixion meant a bloody, violent death. Only the worst criminals were sentenced to die this way. To us, the cross is a shiny crucifix, but to Jesus it was an instrument of torture, humiliation, and death.

■ Pass out 3 x 5" cards and ask your students to write on it -- "He Died For Me." Then ask them to sign their names. They will use the cards later in the lesson.

Key Principle # 3: JESUS CHRIST, GOD'S SON, OFFERS HIS LIFE TO YOU.

■ Spend some time on I John 5:11-13. This is perhaps the clearest passage in the New Testament about who has eternal life and who doesn't. Point out the following truths:

A.   Eternal life is wrapped up in a person -- Jesus Christ (verse 11)

B.   To "have" the Son means to have a personal relationship with Him. (verse 12)

C.   There is a difference between living and having "life." There are many people who are alive who don't have "life." (verse 12)

67

D.   God wants you to know that you are going to heaven. (verse 13)

E.   Believing in Jesus Christ is the same thing as "having" Him. To believe in Jesus is to enter into a personal relationship with Him. (verses 12-13)

F.   Eternal life is something you have right now. (verse 13)

G.   When you enter into a personal relationship with Jesus Christ, at that moment you have eternal life and you can know that you are going to heaven. (verse 13)

H.   Therefore, the most important decision you can ever make is
the decision to enter into a personal relationship with Jesus Christ. It is the decision that makes the difference between life and death, hell and heaven.

■ Make your Gospel appeal as strong as possible. Close by reading the final paragraph of this section.

Key Principle # 4:   JESUS CHRIST, GOD'S SON, WAITS FOR YOU TO RECEIVE HIM.

■ Bridge back to the first point by reminding the students that everyone has a god. The only question is -- Who is your God? Is Jesus Christ your God or are you still following some manmade substitute?

■ After all has been said and done, God leaves the decision with you. What will you do with Jesus Christ? Nothing else is more important.

■ Lead your students through the prayer on page 112. A simple way to do it is as follows: First, read the prayer out loud slowly. Then ask them to consider making that prayer their own. Then ask them to repeat the prayer silently as you read it aloud phrase by phrase.

■ As you finish, go back to I John 5:11-13 and read it again. Ask the students, Where do you find eternal life? (In Jesus Christ) How do you get eternal life? (By believing in Jesus Christ) According to verse 13, what can you know when you put your trust in Jesus? (That you have eternal life)

- Summarize the comments in the concluding paragraph. Congratulate them again on completing the study.

APPLICATION:

- **The "He Died For Me" Project**. The purpose of this project is to help your students come face to face with the reality of Christ dying for them. It turns theory into reality. For those who are just making the decision to trust Jesus as Savior, this project will help cement that decision.

In order to do it, you will need to build a wooden cross that is between 5-6 feet tall. The older and rougher the wood, the better the effect will be. Mount the cross on a secure base so that it will stand alone. Place a hammer and a box of nails at the base.

As you come to the end, ask your students to find those 3 x 5" cards that read "He Died For Me." They should have signed them earlier in the lesson.

Ask the students to come up one by one and nail their cards to the cross. You don't need any music or other commentary. Let the only sound be the sound of the hammer driving the nails into the wood. As one student finishes, another one comes forward. (You as the teacher should go first so the students know exactly what to do.)

- When everyone has finished, sing an appropriate hymn such as "Jesus Paid It All" or a chorus such as "He Paid a Debt He Did Not Owe."

PRAYER:

"Thank you, Lord Jesus, for making God real to us. Thank you for dying so that we might have eternal life. Amen."

Shepherd Ministries
...from Dawson McAllister
ORDER FORM

MANUALS

	STUDENT Price	Code	Qty	TEACHER Price	Code	Qty	TRANSPARENCIES Price	Code	Qty
Student Relationships Volume I	8.75	2010		6.95	2011		43.95	2080	
Student Relationships Volume II	8.75	2012		6.95	2013		43.95	2081	
Student Relationships Volume III	8.75	2014		6.95	2015		43.95	2082	
A Walk With Christ to the Cross	8.95	2030		5.95	2031		24.95	2085	
Through the Resurrection	8.95	2032							
Student Discipleship Volume I	8.50	2020							
Student Discipleship Volume II	8.50	2022							
Who are you, Jesus?	7.95	2040		5.95	2041				
Who is Your God?	7.95	2050		5.95	2051				
You, God, and Your Sexuality	3.95	2060							
Preparing Your Teenager for Sexuality (For Parents)	6.95	2065							
Handbook of Financial Faithfulness	6.95	8010							
Dawson Speaks Out on Self Esteem & Loneliness	3.95	2070							
Search for Significance	7.95	2075							
Conf. Follow-Up Manual	2.95	2055							

Mail completed order blank to:
SHEPHERD MINISTRIES
2845 W. Airport Frwy. Suite 137
Irving, TX 75062
(214) 570-7599

VIDEOS

	PURCHASE Price	Code	Qty
A Walk with Christ to the Cross	189.95	4120	
When Tragedy Strikes	79.95	4740	
Dawson Speaks Out on Self Esteem and Loneliness	169.95	4050	
Christianity in Overalls (4 Part)	169.95	4020	
Straight Talk About Friends and Peer Pressure (5 Part)	169.95	4040	
Student Workbooks (Set of 5)	6.25	4340	
Preparing Your Teenager for Sexuality	189.95	4100	

VIDEOS

	PURCHASE Price	Code	Qty
How to Get Along With Your Parents (4 Sessions)	169.95	4030	
Student Workbooks (Set of 5)	9.75	4330	
Papa, Please Love Me!	169.95	4060	
Tough Questions About Sex	59.95	4010	
Too Young to Die	69.95	4750	
Making Peace with Dad	69.95	4730	
Kids in Crisis	69.95	4720	
Life 101	99.95	4800	

SHIP TO:
Name
Organization
Position
Address
City   State   Zip
Phone (   )

Total Order
Shipping
Total Due

☐ Please bill me
☐ Payment enclosed

For postage & handling: Add 8% of the total amt.; minimum charge - $2.00. For orders over $150.00, please add 5% of the total amt. For special RUSH shipments (2-day UPS or First Class), add 13% of the total; minimum charge — $4.00.